# THE GEAl

*A COMMUNITY & OAK FOREST LOST FOREVER*

*Scéal Beag*
*Trua Mór*

Josephine O'Connell

Published by Googie-Woggie Publishing

First Published 2008

Printed in Ireland by Walsh Printing, Clonakilty, Co. Cork

Copyright reserved

ISBN 0-9560562-0-2

All photographs by the author unless otherwise indicated.
Front cover photograph: Bridget O'Connell
Map sketches: Ellen Barrett

This publication has received support from the Heritage Council under the 2008 Publications Grant Scheme.

Dedicated to
The Oak Trees
&
The People Who Suffered a Heartbreaking Loss

## A Word of Thanks…

In putting together just a small book like this it is amazing how many people help out along the way. I would like to thank all of the following: Denis Shannon, Teresa Buckley and Vaughans of the Café for pointing me in the direction of people that lived in the Gearagh. Micko Kelleher, Joanie Herlihy and Peggy Bradley for their time and wonderful memories. My mother for her spelling and punctuation! Barty for his encouragement and support. Fiona for her enthusiasm and motivation. Phil who knows herself how she helped. Ellen for coming to the rescue when I was in a pinch. Shane, Eddie and the staff of Coláiste Stiofáin Naofa, without whom I would not even have contemplated doing this project. Kevin Corcoran and Seamus O'Donoghue for giving me permission to use extracts from their books. All other sources I availed of. Donal O'Leary for his help with the paper work. Walsh printers in Clonakilty who are a pleasure to deal with. The Heritage Council and CSN for their financial support. If I have not mentioned you personally please forgive me and a special thanks to you all. I would also like to acknowledge the other people who lived in the Gearagh whose stories I was unable to get due to time constraints. Who knows maybe a next edition!

*Best wishes
Josephine O'Connell
21/12/08*

# CONTENTS

Maps . . . . . . . . . . . . . . . . . . . . . . . . . . . . . . . . . . . . . . . . . .6

Introduction . . . . . . . . . . . . . . . . . . . . . . . . . . . . . . . . . .9

How it all began . . . . . . . . . . . . . . . . . . . . . . . . . . . . . .10

The Gearagh before the Flood . . . . . . . . . . . . . . . . . . . . .12

The Community . . . . . . . . . . . . . . . . . . . . . . . . . . . . . .15

An Poitín . . . . . . . . . . . . . . . . . . . . . . . . . . . . . . . . . . .20

Seán Ruad an Gaortaig . . . . . . . . . . . . . . . . . . . . . . . . .21

The Beginning of the End . . . . . . . . . . . . . . . . . . . . . . .23

List of those affected by the flooding in the Gearagh area . . . . .27

Bridges . . . . . . . . . . . . . . . . . . . . . . . . . . . . . . . . . . . .30

Cutting the Trees . . . . . . . . . . . . . . . . . . . . . . . . . . . . .32

Conclusion . . . . . . . . . . . . . . . . . . . . . . . . . . . . . . . . .34

Notes . . . . . . . . . . . . . . . . . . . . . . . . . . . . . . . . . . . . .37

Bibliography . . . . . . . . . . . . . . . . . . . . . . . . . . . . . . . .38

## MAPS (different scale)

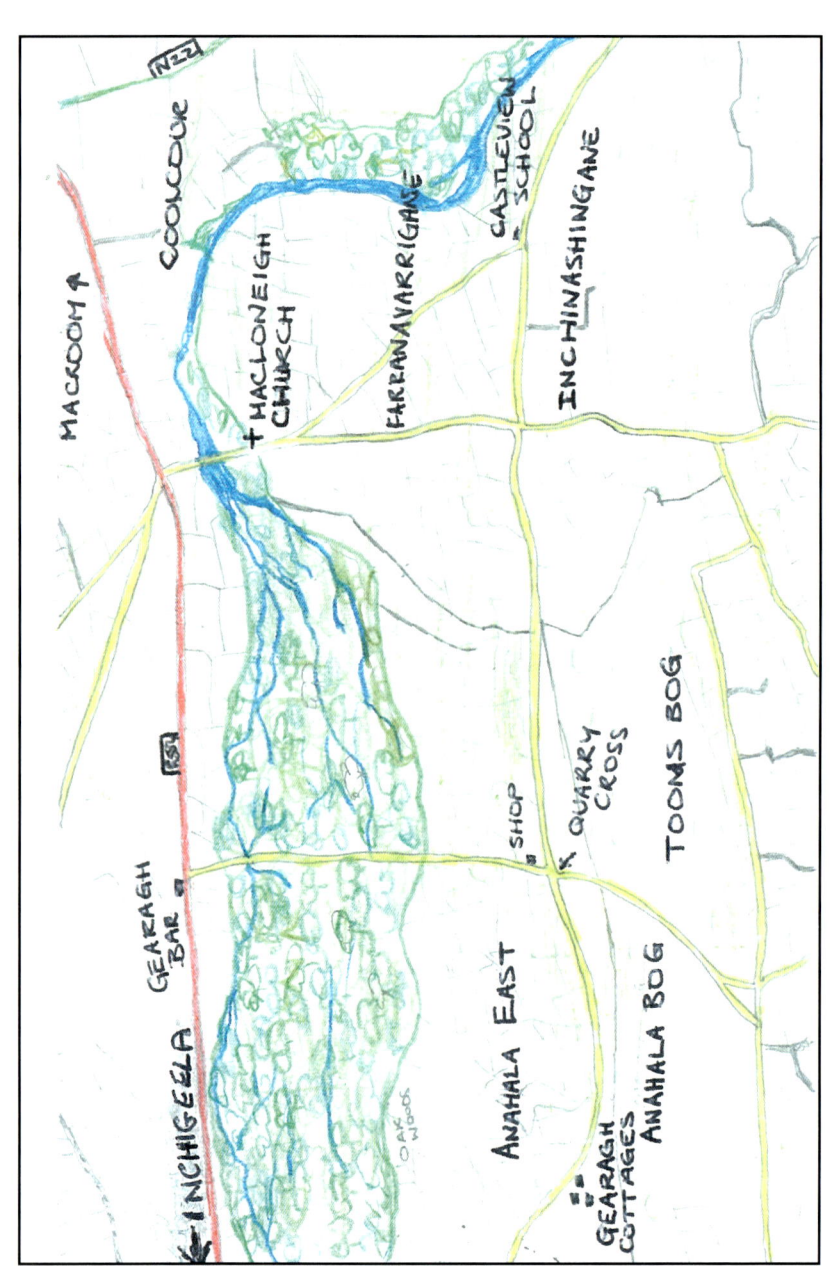

BEFORE......

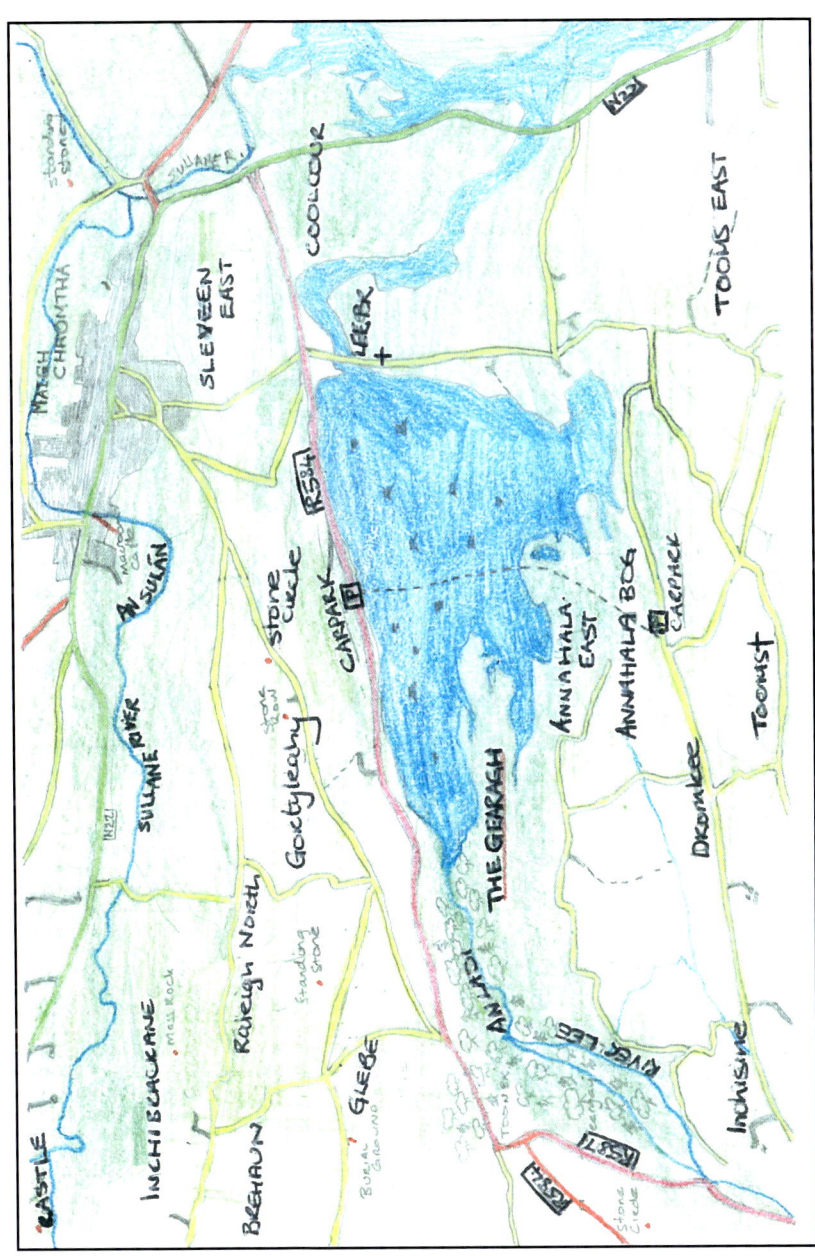

......and AFTER

# INTRODUCTION

When deciding to do a local history project it was difficult to choose a topic as the area I come from, mid Cork, is steeped in history. I decided on the Gearagh, because having lived in Macroom for ten years, it is practically on my doorstep. For people living in Macroom the Gearagh is like an extension of their back garden because it is so accessible for pleasant nature walks. It is situated less than a mile as the crow flies south over Slaveen hill from the town. It is approximately two and a half miles out the main flat R584 road to Inchigeela/ Dunmanway. It includes the town lands of Annahala East and West and is bounded by Farranavarrigane, Inchisine, Inchinashingane and Tooms (that were in the old parish of Maconleigh) and Teergay, as well as Raleigh South, Tullatreada and Slaveen West that are north of the main road.

Having passed by it several times on the road and gone for many wonderful walks in it, the Gearagh always held a sense of wonder and intrigue for me. That being said I never knew exactly what it's story was. To the uninformed passer-by (myself included) it is a large lake on the River Lee with peculiar black tree stumps, barely visible when the water level is high. Mysteriously at times the water level completely drops, revealing these stumps in their entirety, and the mud from which they protrude. This changing water level had been familiar to me since my childhood as I travelled by bus to secondary school in Macroom for five years. This trip from Aghabullogue via Coachford and Carrigadrohid along the Lee Valley gave me constant access to viewing the changes in height of the water level of the river. Although at the time I knew 'The Dam' was responsible for this, I never investigated the severity of the impact of this famous dam, which is in actual fact, two dams……

The Gearagh at dusk                          *(photo P O'Connell)*

## HOW IT ALL BEGAN

In February 1953 work began on the construction of the Inniscarra dam. May of the same year saw the commencement of work on the Carrigadrohid dam. They were both completed towards the end of 1956.[1] An article in the Cork Examiner dated Wednesday 24th October 1956 entitled 'Flooding of Upper Part of Lee Valley Begins' subheading 'Plan To Bring Reservoir To Low Water Level in Eight Days' reports: "Yesterday was a momentous day in the development of the Hydro-Electric Scheme on the River Lee, when unostentatiously and without ceremony, the flooding of the upper part of the Lee Valley was begun. One of the sluices in the dam at Carrigadrohid, 20 miles from Cork, was partially closed to restrict the flow of water and, imperceptibly the water from there back towards the river's source began to rise. In a period of eight days it is planned to bring the new reservoir on the Lee to its low water level. This means rising the level of the water at the upriver side of the Carrigadrohid dam by a matter of some 33 feet. The level will then be 200 feet above sealevel."[2]

THE CORK EXAMINER, WEDNESDAY, OCTOBER 24, 1956

# Flooding Of Lee Valley

LEE HYDRO-ELECTRIC SCHEME—The dam at Carrigadrohid, Co. Cork, which is expected to be completed in the spring. The flooding of the Lee Valley began yesterday when one of the sluices in the dam was raised to restrict the flow of water.

In the same paper on October 27th an article headed 'Lee Waters Will Soon Cover The Gearagh' states that: "When the waters will cover the Gearagh is not quite decided…. The high water level will be 15 feet above the low level and that will put a very great area under water. It will take the lake back along the Sullane River as far as the bridge a mile from Macroom on the Cork – Coachford – Macroom road and to the south to the slopes of the big road diversion made by the E.S.B. near Toames East."[3] Apparently the local women gathered on Slaveen Hill and wept as they watched their beloved Gearagh being submerged. It was a proper wake!

# THE GEARAGH BEFORE THE FLOOD

Although the same Cork Examiner reports that the scene had been well recorded: ("Before a single sod was turned, the Cork Camera Club completed a very fine film in colour of the river from source to sea") I have been unable to get any photographs of the woodland area of the Gearagh and as Kevin Corcoran admits in his very informative book 'West Cork Walks': "It is hard to imagine what the Gearagh looked like before being flooded."[4] In an attempt to create a picture of what it was like, I have gathered as many descriptions as possible:

"The Gearagh is a strange place. The name is applied to a tract of land about four miles long and one mile wide at its broadest point. It is practically flat and marshy from end to end. A road runs from north to south across its middle and a few cottages straddled this route. Another few homes lie further to the west in the Annahala end of the Gearagh. …little streams and wildfowl-haunted lakes abounded in this wilderness as they have done since time immemorial."[5]

" …the area could best be described as an immense marsh, overgrown with sallies, alder, small ash and elm trees, with an undergrowth of sedge and rushes. The name itself is derived from the Irish word *gaorthadh*, a river shrubbery."[6]

"Above Macroom, where the stream runs through flat meadows, it spreads out, dividing and rejoining again and again, among trees and bushes, forming a delightful combination of wood and clear swift water – a very curious feature, and unique in Ireland. The place is suitably called The Gearagh (*Gaertha*, a woodland along a river) and is well worth exploring in one of the flat-bottomed boats which are in use for this purpose."[7]

(Photo from Ballingeary Historical Society Journal 2000)   *Photo R E Hadden*

"At Toon Bridge commences that unique stretch of the Lee, the Gearagh. From the roadside all you can see is a wilderness of small trees, mostly alder, and reeds with an occasional gleam of water. The Gearagh is a complex of river channels running through this vegetation, a miniature Florida swamp about three miles long. From Sleveen Hill over Macroom you can get a general view of this wilderness and there is also a road crossing it about half-way between Toon Bridge and Sleveen East. This road passes across a half a mile of the Gearagh and seems to be a series of little bridges. From these you can look up and down quietly running streams, where often a flotilla of ducks sail across or heron is seen motionless between the reeds. It's a lonely place to find a river. You expect to see Red Indians come down in a canoe or aquatic monsters nosing around in the dark shades beneath the alders." [8]

"This country was all a forest. The woods consisted of large oak, birch, alder some ash and many yews of as great a bulk as the largest oak. Great quantities of fir are still taken out of the turf bogs. This forest was then stored with red and fallow deer and abounded with great eyries of excellent hawks."9

" ... and from four to five miles in breadth from north to south, lies a tract called Gearagh. This tract evidently formed the bed of a lake subsequently silted up, but at the beginning of the eighteenth century and for along time afterwards it was a wilderness of bog, alluvial islands, deep pools, tangled underwood, and large trees, and was one of the last refuges of the wolf and the bittern in the South of Ireland. It was much subject to floods, and for more than half the year was practically unpassable."10

Starting to explore the Gearagh

Photo: R. Welch

(Photo from BHSJ 2000)

"It was until the 1950s a post-glacial, alluvial oak river-forest. Here was a place where time itself stood still. The Gearagh had remained unchanged since its formation ten thousand years previously, at the end of the last Ice Age. – a vast inland delta of inter-connecting, many branched streams that encircled a maze of small and inaccessible islands, covered in oak forest. It was protected from the ravages of humanity by its swampy terrain, deep swirling streams and treacherous banks of soft muds with holes big enough to swallow a horse."11

"This river has its course here, interrupted with islands and a deep boggy tract, until it runs to the bridge of Ballynaclassen. These islands are covered, mostly with oak, ash, hazel and birch; at the feet of which grow fern, polypodium, and water drop worth. Here are great quantities of several kinds of waterfowl, in their season, as bitterns, cranes, duck and mallard, teal, &c.. These bogs have been attempted to be drained, but it was found impracticable. In one called Anaghaly, is about three acres of ground, on which is excellent limestone, that supplies the town of Macroom, the western inhabitants of this barony and Carbery, with lime for manure and building."[12]

Although these accounts vary slightly, we are left in no doubt about the magic and uniqueness of the Gearagh. Much has been written on the wonderful, natural haven that it was, and still is for wildlife, however very little has been recorded about the people and their ancestors who lived there for generations, and how they lost their homes.

## THE COMMUNITY

The following account of life in the Gearagh is derived primarily from interviews with Mrs Joanie Herlihy (nee Cronin) who lives in Dromkeen and Micko Kelleher living in Masseytown. They were both born and reared in the Gearagh and recall very happy memories of their childhood and growing up in total harmony with nature in this idyllic place, where there was "every kind of a tree, every kind of a plant, every kind of a flower, every kind of a bird and frogs galore." In summer time it was like having their own private seaside and they swam in 'Ling a Pholaig'.

In the first half of the twentieth century, the Gearagh Community consisted of twenty four houses and one shop. This shop, owned by Horgans, was 'a beautiful place with a garden' and sold 'everything'; groceries, meal, flour as well as paraffin. It was located at the Quarry Cross which can still be identified. It is the "main" crossroads in the Gearagh about half a mile south, straight in from the car park on the main Inchigeela road. The Horgans dwelling house was beside the shop. There were four more houses near the cross, owned by Kellehers, Henigans, Tobins and O'Riordans, also living in Annahala East were Buttimers, Richard Cronin and Tommy Murphys. The remainder of the houses were scattered west along the road from the Quarry Cross, in Annahala West. These were the properties of Jack Creed, Tommy Murray, Sheehans, Rings, Tom Shea, O'Learys, Bradleys, Cronins, Neilus Lucey, Blakes, Stephen Creedon, Mannings, Kearneys, Jeffers, Murphys and Kellehers. There was also a public house called 'The Gearagh Bar' owned by Cashmans, across the road from the car park mentioned above.

Children living in the Gearagh had a choice of two national schools, Castleview and Tooms, both of which were about a two mile walk away. Mrs. Herlihy fondly recalls how the different children used to leave stones at the Quarry Cross to let the others know if they were already gone. There were regular games of football, sometimes as many as twenty three a side (forty six in total). This was a huge crowd of youngsters who must have come from miles around. Another game they played was throwing 'quaits' which was like 'pitch and toss' except stones were used instead of coins. Bowling was also popular.

Micko Kelleher, whose family moved to Masseytown.

Mrs Joanie Herlihy (standing) and Mrs Peggy Bradley, who both grew up in The Gearagh. Photo taken in Bradleys house which survived.

The 'happiest families ever' were living in The Gearagh and there was never a falling out. It was generally a farming community and everybody helped each other with the planting and digging of the potatoes, the cutting and threshing of corn as well as saving the hay. Kellehers had six cows which generally had 'the run of' The Gearagh, except for some forbidden areas. It was Micko's job on occasions to look after them. On one such occasion Micko got distracted, as any young fellow does, and went off caffling with his mates. On his return he found his cows happily grazing in a 'no go zone'. Lo and behold the smell of the milk was so strong that the creamery refused to accept it. The cows had filled their bellies with *'cnumh'* which is a type of wild garlic. There was 'blue war' and Micko didn't get caught dossing again in a hurry!

It was a great place for fishing and shooting and there was never a shortage of game. Tommy Murphy, better known as Tommy Tom owned a boat and took people for sporting as well as recreational trips. He was a 'top notch boat man' and could find his way around The Gearagh in the dark from Toons Bridge to Macloneigh.

Tommy Tom also owned a gramophone which provided much entertainment in the evenings. There was a platform in Toons Bridge and groups went across country through the river to get to the dances. They used *'cosaí fuara'*, which were a type of short hazel stilt, a bit like old fashioned wooden crutches that come up to the 'oxter', with a step halfway up, to keep the feet dry. Mrs. Herlihy's father, Tadhg Cronin, specialized in making these. There was an art in using them and more often than not 'the acrobats' fell into the water!

The Quarry Cross which was the centre of the Gearagh community.

Micko tells of how Dan Cotter, who worked for Dinny Riordan, owned a pet fox. This fox was a major attraction and people came from all around to see him. One day when people came, there was no trace of the fox. Dan was in a fix. He couldn't understand where his beloved fox had disappeared to. When the gang were gone the fox reappeared, mysteriously! The 'painted devils' had pushed the fox up the chimney, (there was no fire lighting) and blocked him up there with a bag, just for 'the crack'.

The 'Port' Road from The Quarry Cross to Johno's (Kelleher) Cross which the children would have walked going to Castleview school.

"At one time the Gearaghs were also famous for the production of a high quality brand of potheen, consignments of which travelled far and wide, even across the Atlantic. It is said the distillers were kept busy filling orders for the wedding, the wake, the threshing and the Christmas festivities. Transport difficulties were often experienced, but ingenious methods were devised which saw supplies frequently despatched by way of the creel of turf, the firkin of butter, or concealed in a bag of oats."[13]

"The Gearagh was a great haunt of poteen makers and hard work it was to catch anyone in this mixture of land and water." [14] It was believed that any stranger (including the guardians of the law) that did not have the best interest of the locals at heart, fell victim of a phenomenon known as *'Jackie the Lantern'* or in Irish *'meascán mearaí'*, when they entered the Gearagh. This was a state of bewilderment that left them totally confused and without any sense of direction! (The cure for this condition is to turn your coat inside out!)

## AN POITÍN by Seoirse Seartan, Ballingeary (translation)[15]

The poets of Munster from Bantry to Brugh,
Made verses in praise of the Mountain Dew,
How a glass would give strength to the halt and the lame,
And bring beauty and youth to the tottering dame.

Said O'Donnell "No poet am I it is true,
But I made many a jar of the horrible brew,
And here's the re-action of drinking it neat,
With the flavour of moth and the smell of the peat.

The hunchback imagines he's as big as a giant,
The dwarf has grown up to be bold and defiant,
The lame and the deaf became active and keen,
And the hag by the fireside thinks she's the Queen.

The daisy is a sun-flower, the calf is a cow,
Every duck is a swan, every slip is a sow,
The ember's a bonfire, the chaff weighs a pound,
And the shaft of the spade stands ten feet from the ground.

The dross from the smithy piled up by the sty,
Is Mangerton Mountain with peak in the sky,
The ooze of the resin from larchwood and pine,
Is a river of amber as wide as the Rhine.

This powerful potheen bringing death or a cure,
Kills beetles and bugs if applied immature,
A drop would if taken the day of the chase,
Make a buck-rabbit spit in a terrier's face."

The Gearagh boasts many characters, none more famous than Sean Rua (red haired John), the Rapparee. He also benefited from the *'meascán mearaí'* that befell his pursuers! This version of his heroics is taken from the National Folklore Collection, Toames National School 1937-8.

(NFC S.338: 216-7, reproduced with courtesy of the National Folklore Collection, University College Dublin.)

## Seán Ruad an Gaortaig
*Story by Denis Lane (Farmer), Mountmusic, Toames, Macroom (age 50)*

Tradition tells us, that over two hundred years ago there dwelt a famous rapparee in the banks of the Lee between Macroom and Kilmichael named "Seán Ruad an Gaortaig". He was no enemy to the peasantry, but at that time the country was overruled by tyrannical landlords and this man robbed the rich to serve the poor.

The British military were constantly in search of him, but, he cleverly evaded capture each time. One night, as he was seated in one of his secret huts in the Gearah he narrowly escaped being captured, as an armed band of British military suddenly approached the hut. Sean, however, quickly thought of a trick and he seized a wheel that lay in the hut and rolled it down the pathway in front of the house in the direction of the military, who were amazed and stunned for the time being. While they stood gazing at this, Sean made his escape by an exit the opposite way and was lost sight of in the pathways so well known to "Sean Ruad".

He was a wonderful shot: For instance, when Hedges White the owner of Macroom castle and some of his loyal friends were dining within the castle on a certain night Sean came about mid-night, and discharged a shot from his gun whilst he stood outside the castle and quenched the candle which was lighting near by on the dining table which naturally terrorised them.

*Soon afterwards there was and officer who was a famous shot brought to Macroom to join the other military there in pursuit of Sean. This man boasted, that if he caught sight of a square inch of the rapparee he would have him either dead or alive. This resulted in a two days pardon given to "Sean Ruad" in order to meet his opponent in the square of Macroom in order to have a trial test as to which of them would be the better shot.*

*Hundreds thronged the town on that day and about two o'clock, up walked "Sean Ruad" fully armed and equipped. Then the trial began. A crown piece was placed on the castle wall which was shot off by "Sean Ruad" and the officer in quick succession. Then a penknife was placed on the wall with a similar result. Sean then took a penknife from his pocket and placed it edge forward on the wall. The officer fired, and missed by a narrow margin. Then came Sean Ruad fired quickly. The referee was astonished to find the bullet stuck in the board behind the knife, split evenly in two. He thus declared Sean Ruad the winner. When the crowd filled in to witness the scene the rapparee disappeared as quickly he came to again live as before, the life of an outlaw. He was never caught, as it is related that he died in his bed. His real name was John Sullivan, and some people boast of being blood relations of his. It is said that he is the author of that famous song called "The Flourishing States of Kilmurry".*

A much more elaborate version of this story, entitled 'Shawn Ru, the Rapparee: a Tradition of Macroom' can be found in a Journal of the Cork Historical and Archaeological Society. It was written by 'An Old Inhabitant' and many more of Sean's heroic deeds are outlined. It also states that Sean's name was Murphy as distinct from Sullivan and ends like this:

"Whether Mr. Hedges made any specific arrangement with Shawn Ru at the time of the shooting match is left to conjecture; but Shawn Ru settled down at his house at Terelton shortly afterwards, and the yeomen looked after him no more. He visited Macroom whenever he thought proper, and no one ever attempted to molest him. Though married, as already stated, he had no children. He lived long beyond the span usually allotted to man and died calmly in his bed.

The peasantry at the south side of Gaeragh long treasured his memory. A song in the Irish language, each stanza of which ended with 'Maw's mough lath veh boon, caugh foor augus theh,' was composed in his honour; and down to the time of the famine in '46 could be met many people who spoke of him as a hero, and related almost with pride of a personal achievement Shawn Ru's victory over the Hessian by the shot that made his fame."[16] This Anglisized Irish line loosely translates as 'if you want to be lasting you must flee.'

## *THE BEGINNING OF THE END*

In the early fifties a man named Buckley who worked with the ESB arrived from Dublin in a 'big car'. He went around from house to house knocking on doors, offering the owners money for their property. Initially people didn't believe their ears. How could this happen? How could their homes, the homes of their ancestors for generations before them, be bought out from under them? Unlike today, people felt powerless and there was no organized campaign of protest. Buckley came back week after week raising the offer slightly until eventually people gave in, knowing that they had no choice but to sell. The harsh reality struck. There was no fixed rate and most people were not at all satisfied with the deal. They took what they got because they felt they had no choice as the flooding was going to go ahead regardless.

Horgans of the shop were the first to leave. They went to Ballincollig, where they set up shop again, but sadly Mr. Horgan died soon afterwards, it is said of a broken heart. After Horgans, people left their houses one by one, took their belongings and headed to various destinations. Three council cottages were provided in Dooniskey, Lissarda. Some people moved in to Macroom town, more just scattered and most farmers that lost their homesteads bought land wherever they could get it.

A DOOMED HOME—The Kelliher family leave this house in the Gearagh to-day, for soon this big tract of flat land will be flooded to feed the generating station at Carrigadrohid.

# Lee Waters Will Soon Cover The Gearagh

### Families Prepare To Leave Their Homes— But Some Have Nowhere To Go

The Cork Examiner of Saturday October 27th 1956 reported:

"As the waters of the upper reaches of the River Lee rose slowly yesterday in Carrigadrohid reservoir flooding inhabitants of the Gearagh district which lies to the south of Macroom prepared to leave their homes. Their homelands are not flooded – yet. Some of the families have left and are established in their new homes. Some are on their way. Some have nowhere to go.

An Examiner reporter who travelled the north Cork-Macroom road

"I have nowhere to go." said Mr. Daniel Cotter, a 65-year-old I.R.A. pensioner, to our reporter. The friend's house in which he lived has been pulled down.

yesterday to see the new lake rising near Caum, (three or four miles on the Cork side of Macroom), travelled further west to the Gearagh and there talked to the people who are clinging to their old homesteads until the eleventh hour.

From the flat terrain, newly created ruins stuck out like sore thumbs.

As cottages were abandoned by their owners, the slates were pulled off the roofs and, in some cases, walls tumbled in. In one instance, that of the Gearagh's sole shop only the concrete floor and foundation remains.

But wisps of smoke still trickled from a few chimneys early yesterday afternoon.

One of the first houses entered by our reporter was that of Mr and Mrs James Kelleher. They have a family of five*. They move out today and yesterday were preparing to shift all their belongings. Neighbours gave a helping hand. Less than a stone's throw almost in the backyard – is a lake."[17]

In the heart of the Gearagh, a marshy flat district south of Macroom, houses are being abandoned and pulled down, for the land will go under water in the Lee Hydro-electric Scheme. This picture shows some of the partly-demolished houses and the still tenanted home of the Misses Tobin.

Site of demolished house.

Some of the older inhabitants of the twenty four houses mentioned in the previous section had died before the flooding. Some of the houses are still standing. These include Cronins, Bradleys, Neilus Luceys (now occupied by Tom Heffernan) and Tommy Murphys. All the other houses were demolished, including 'The Gearagh Bar' which never got flooded. For the people that were left it was extremely sad, as not only had they lost their wonderful neighbours but they also had, and still have, a constant reminder of the destruction that was done. As well as that they had been distanced from their local town of Macroom. What until then had been little more than a two mile walk across the Gearagh and over Slaveen hill, suddenly became a seven or eight mile journey by road around the flooded area. This was a serious inconvenience, especially as motor cars were extremely scarce at the time.

Gatepost that escaped!

The following statistics are taken from The Appendix of Seamus O'Donoghue's in-depth study, *The Flooding of the Lee Valley* p85 to 95. They have been rearranged and put in townland order. The names in **bold** print denote the dwellings acquired by the ESB.

### LIST OF THOSE AFFECTED BY THE FLOODING IN THE GEARAGH AREA.

| NAME | TOWNLAND | AREA ACQUIRED<br>a – r – sq pers. |
|---|---|---|
| Mrs. Bradley | Annahala Bog | 1 – 0 - 23 |
| **Patrick J. Buttimer** | **Annahala Bog** | 61 – 1 - 13 |
|  | Annahala East | 9 – 1 - 27 |
| Mrs. Kate Godsil | Dromkeen, Annahalabog | 89 – 3 - 20 |
| Denis T. Murphy | Annahala Bog | 44 – 2 - 27 |
|  | Annahala East | 0 – 2 - 13 |
| **Thos P. Murphy** | **Annahala East** & Annahala Bog | 243 – 2 - 37 |
| **Richard Cronin** | **Annahala East** | _____ |

| | | |
|---|---|---|
| J. Hennigan | **Annahala East** | 1 – 0 - 20 |
| **John Horgan** | **Annahala East** | 5 – 3 - 32 |
| **James Kelleher** | **Annahala East** | 7 – 2 - 6 |
| Cornelius Manning | Annahala East | 1 – 1 - 0 |
| **Denis O'Riordan** | **Annahala East** | 45 – 3 – 30 |
| | | 2 – 0 - 21 |
| **Miss N. Tobin** | **Annahala East** | 1 – 0 - 19 |
| Mrs. Julia Blake | Annahala West | 23 – 0 - 23 |
| **Mrs. Margt. Creedon** | **Annahala West,** Gearagh | 53 – 3 - 16 |
| (Reps.) Timothy Cronin | | |
| Daniel Cronin | Annahala West | _____ |
| **James Kearney** (Labourer's Plot) **Annahala West** | | |
| Daniel Kelleher | Gearagh West, Annahala West | 77 – 0 - 7 |
| Cornelius Lucey | Annahala West, Annahala Bog | 4 – 2 – 31 |
| **Daniel Manning** | **Annahala West** | 0 – 2 - 2 |
| **Thos. T. Murphy** | **Annahala West** | 1 – 3 - 14 |
| | Gearagh East | 65 – 0 – 8 |
| Timothy Murphy | Annahala West | 35 – 0 - 25 |
| | Geagagh West | 8 – 0 - 34 |
| Wm. O'Driscoll | Annahala West | 0 – 2 - 2 |
| Jeremiah O'Leary | Annahala West | 40 – 1 - 30 |
| Thomas O'Shea | Annahala West | 30 – 1 - 19 |
| | Annahala Bog | 11 – 2 - 37 |
| James O'Mahony | Farranavarrigane | 27 – 1 - 26 |
| Denis Cronin | Farranavarrigane | 13 – 2 - 25 |
| John Buckley | Inchinashingane | 8 – 1 - 31 |
| John Dennehy | Inchinashingane | |
| Cornelius Desmond | Inchinashingane | _____ |
| John Kelleher | Inchinashingane | 33 – 0 - 26 |
| (Reps) Patk. J. Murphy | Inchinashingane | 0 – 2 - 37 |
| Timothy Murphy | Inchinashingane | 27 – 2 - 3 |
| | Do (Addtl.) | 3 – 2 - 0 |

| | | |
|---|---|---|
| (Reps) C.O'Callaghan | | |
| John O'Riordan | Inchinashingane | 6 – 0 - 6 |
| Mrs. Nellie Browne | Raleigh South | 57 – 1 – 4 |
| Daniel Kelleher | Raleigh South | 23 – 1 - 8 |
| Jeremiah Creedon | Slaveen East | 9 – 3 - 28 |
| John Lynch | Slaveen East | 5 – 1 - 8 |
| | water | 2 – 1 - 7 |
| Cornelius Lucey | Slaveen West | 42 – 1 - 21 |
| Cornelius Murray | Slaveen West | 43 – 1 - 24 |
| | (Inc. half of river) | |
| Mrs. H. Nicholls | Teergay | 34 – 2 - 27 |
| Earl of Bandon | Tooms Bog | 108 – 3 - 35 |
| Patk. O'Sullivan | Tooms Bog | 10 – 0 - 15 |
| Mrs. B. Cullinane | Tooms E. Dunisky | 19 – 0 - 28 |
| Michael Buckley | Tooms West | 2 – 1 - 17 |
| (Reps) James Cronin | Tooms West | 0 – 0 - 14 |
| Denis Horgan | | (Dist. loss of spring well etc.) |
| Jeremiah McSweeney | Tooms West | 15 – 3 - 29 |
| | Tooms Bog | 2 – 0 - 15 |
| John McSweeney | Tooms West | 1 – 1 - 9 |
| Patk. O'Mahony | Tooms West | 5 – 1 - 34 |
| **Jeremiah Cashman** | **Tullatreada** | 16 – 2 - 32 |
| John Buckley | Tullatreada | 0 – 2 - 35 |
| Mrs. H A. Cashman | Tullatreada | 0 – 0 - 34 |
| **Denis Cotter** | **Tullatreada** | 0 – 1 - 36 |
| Daniel Creedon | Tullatreada | 0 – 0 - 24 |
| Timothy Creedon | Tullatreada | 16 – 1 - 8 |
| John Lordan | Tullatreada | |
| Edward Meaney | Tullatreada | 101 – 2 - 20 |
| Mrs. M. O'Riordan | Tullatreada | 2 – 2 – 18 |

**TOTAL: 1511 acres    2 roods    11 perches**[2]

The New Bridge

Annahala Bridge

The Small Arch

The four bridges between The Quarry Cross and The Gearagh Bar

## CUTTING THE TREES

"All scrub and trees growing below the high water level in the reservoirs were cut to the extent that no tree would project within five feet of the low water level. The Gearagh, covering about 250 acres, was made up of many islands divided by narrow river channels. The ESB had great difficulty in getting to many of these islands as the river channels were too shallow even for ordinary sailing boats. However, the problem was solved by using ship's life rafts. All this clearing of scrub and non-commercial timber was done by the Board's staff, while commercial timber plantations were sold to timber merchants."[18]

The stumps are completely visible when the water level is low.

Many local lads as well as Macrompian 'old timers' were employed by the ESB to do this deforestation. As Micko admits money was very scarce, and at the time people were a bit innocent and didn't know any better. He recalls a very funny incident which happened on a Monday morning: A colleague of his, having had 'a few too many' the night before arrived to work in a bit of a state. The general consensus was that the best plan was for him to go into one of the piles of scrub and sleep it off. As soon as he was nested down and sleeping peacefully, Dennehy the engineer arrived in his sports car to oversee progress. He got the bright idea that these piles of scrub should be burned. Of course he headed straight for the pile that our friend was neatly concealed in, with matches at the ready. 'The boys had one hell of a job' to distract him and come up with some wonderful idea why this particular pile shouldn't be burnt, although it looked the driest. However they managed and luckily nobody was burned alive!

Every kind of a cutting implement was used in the campaign, including hatchets, slashers, bow saws, cross cuts and the first chain saws, which were operated by two men. These had two handles at one end and one at the other, dangerous sounding weapons! The whole process took about three and a half years, the same length of time as it took to build the dams. Everything was wiped out except one old oak tree which was spared and I believe is still standing today. It is said to be about two hundred years old.

'An uprooted stump'   *(photo P O'Connell)*

Swans Enjoy!

## *CONCLUSION*

It is hard to believe that this tragedy happened just fifty years ago, and got so little public recognition or objection. If the likes were suggested today there would be complete uproar.

In his book Seamus O'Donoghue outlines the criteria necessary for harnessing a river, to successfully operate a hydro electric scheme. They are as follows:
(a) Suitable Location for a dam: A narrow valley or gorge and a suitable rock foundation.
(b) Large River Catchment Area: A good all year round water supply.
(c) A Head of Water: This is determined by the gradient of the river.
(d) Minimum Disruption of the Local Community: Minamal loss of land and human habitation.[19]
Although Inniscarra fulfils most of these criteria, questions have to be asked about the suitability of Carrigadrohid. It is certainly not a v-shaped valley, as a matter of fact the land couldn't be much flatter than the area upriver from Carrigadrohid so the water just spread out over miles. Not only was a

whole community wiped out in the Gearagh but the communities, on both banks of the River Lee from Inniscarra to Toons Bridge, that were close neighbours before the flooding, as there were many crossing points on the river, suddenly became separated by vast stretches of water. How terribly sad!

To end on a more positive note I am once again going to quote Kevin Corcoran, acknowledging the power and wonder of nature:

*"Because the Gearagh was left to nature after being flooded, and not further tampered with, many of the plant species that had formerly occupied the ancient forest began to re-emerge from seed, recolonising the marshy tracts and severed islands. Newly formed lagoons became sanctuaries for rare aquatic species that were being destroyed elsewhere, while the broad sheets of shallow water became a haven for migrant fowl, whose natural habitats are being vandalised by modern agriculture, industrial waste and ignorant developments. Defiantly, the trees too have begun to re-colonise the islands at the top of the reservoir, to form a water-locked, swampy woodland.*
*We have thus been given a second chance to protect the last fragment of our once extensive post-glacial, alluvial forests that cloaked much of the island of Ireland and a large part of mainland Europe, before the arrival of humans. It is imperative that the Gearagh be protected from any further abuse, such as indiscriminate tourism and bungalow developments. Hopefully we have learned our mistake and will take up the challenge."*[20]

AND SO SAY ALL OF US!

# Pretty flowers add colour and life to The Gearagh

Marsh Marigold

Indian Balm  *(photo Anne Hanley)*

# NOTES

1. Seamus O'Donoghue, *The Flooding of the Lee Valley* (Tower Books, Cork, 1996) p97&105.
2. *The Cork Examiner*, 24 October 1956.
3. *The Cork Examiner*, 27 October 1956.
4. Kevin Corcoran, *West Cork Walks* (O'Brien Press, Dublin, 1991) p12.
5. *The Cork Examiner*, 27 October 1956.
6. Liam Milner, *The River Lee And Its Tributaries* (Tower Books, Cork, 1975) p24.
7. Robert Llyod Praeger, *The Way That I Went* (1st pub. 1937, The Collins Press, Cork, 1997) p338.
8. J. C. Coleman, *Journeys into Muskerry* (Dundalgan Press, Dundalk 1950) p23.
9. Donnchadh Ó Luasaigh, 'Dúthaigh an Ghaorthaidh' in *Ballingeary Historical Society Journal* (2000) p9.
10. An Old Inhabitant, 'Shawn Ru, The Rapparee: a Tradition of Macroom' in *Journal of the Cork Historical and Archaeological Society* (1905) p68.
11. Corcoran, *West Cork Walks* p12.
12. Kieran McCarthy, *In the Steps of St. Finbarre* (Nonsuch Publishing, Dublin, 2006) p75.
13. Milner, *The River Lee* p25.
14. Coleman, *Jorneys into Muskerry* p23.
15. Milner, *The River Lee* p25-27.
16. An Old Inhabitant, 'Shawn Ru, The Rapparee' in *JCHAS* p79.
17. *The Cork Examiner*, 27 October 1956. * should have read 'they have a family of six'
18. O'Donoghue, *The Flooding* p84.
19. O'Donoghue, *The Flooding* p40-41.
20. Corcoran, *West Cork Walks* p12-13.

## BIBLIOGRAPHY

*Ballingeary Historical Society Journal,* 2000.
Coleman, J. C., *Journeys into Muskerry,* Dundalgan Press, Dundalk, 1950.
Corcoran, Kevin, *West Cork Walks,* O'Brien Press, Dublin, 1991.
*Journal of the Cork Historical and Archaeological Society,* 1905.
Llyod Praeger, Robert, *The Way That I Went* (1st published 1937) The Collins Press, Cork, 1997.
McCarthy, Kieran, *In the Steps of St. Finbarre,* Nonsuch Publishing, Dublin, 2006.
Milner, Liam, *The River Lee And Its Tributaries,* Tower Books, Cork, 1975.
National Folklore Collection, National Schools Manuscript Collection, 1937-38.
O'Donoghue, Seamus, *The Flooding of the Lee Valley,* Tower Books, Cork, 1996.
*The Cork Examiner* 24 & 27 October 1956.

# Cultural & Heritage Studies

Tramore Road, Cork

*Keeping Tradition Alive!*

Coláiste Stiofáin Naofa, College of Further Education, Tramore Road, Cork offers full-time and part-time programmes of study in Local History, Folklore, Archaeology, English with computer skills and languages along with extensive and interesting weekly field-trips. Anyone intersted in this course of study should contact Shane Lehane @ 021-4969069 or shane@csn.ie

*Living Tradition Project 2008: Building a Dunfanaghy Currach*

# THE HOODED CLOAK

A working cloak worn by women for centuries in Macroom, Kinsale, Skibbereen, Carbery, Killarney and other parts of Munster.

*An awesome garment, suitable for any occasion, now revived and available to you in your choice of colour and fabric.*

A cloak made personally for you by Bridget O'Connell
brighidtrean@yahoo.com
071-9189286    086-3625036